Whittle

1907 – 1996

Warwickshire's Genius of the Jet

by Paul Bolitho

Warwickshire County Council

First published 1998
by
Warwickshire County Council
Department of Planning, Transport & Economic Strategy

ISBN: 1 871942-17-9

Printed in Great Britain by Reynolds Press, Coventry

Contents

Where It All Happened

Key

1	**Coventry** Born 1 June 1907	11	**Lutterworth** The Ladywood Works
2	**Cranwell** RAF College. First Flight E28	12	**Rugby** Brownsover Hall. Design HQ
3	**Hornchurch** 111 Fighter Squadron 1928	13	**Whetstone** Power Jets new factory
4	**Wittering** Central Flying School 1929	14	**Bruntingthorpe** Research & Development Test Flying Aerodrome. Whittle first flew Meteor 1
5	**Digby** 2 Flying Training School 1929	15	**Gloucester** Hucclecote. E28 test flights
6	**Hendon** RAF Display. Crazy flying	16	**Barnoldswick** Rover factory taken over by Rolls Royce
7	**Felixstowe** Marine aircraft testing 1931-2	17	**Edgehill** Flight testing of E28
8	**Henlow** Officers' School of Engineering 1932	18	**Manston** Whittle flew Meteor III High Speed Course. Herne Bay
9	**Cambridge** University (Peterhouse)		
10	**Rugby** BTH Works First run of jet engine, April 12th 1937		

INTRODUCTION

On April 12th 1937 the world's first jet engine was run on a test bed in the British Thomson-Houston factory in Rugby. The jet age had begun! The man who made it possible was Coventry-born engineer, Sir Frank Whittle, "father of the jet engine," arguably the greatest figure Warwickshire has produced in the twentieth century. He had to battle against official indifference and commercial sharp practice for many years, yet he produced a machine which would revolutionise the aviation industry throughout the world and make world wide travel available to ordinary people.

© Ministry of Defence

Whittle – famous overnight

Coventry

Frank Whittle was born on 1st June 1907 at 72 Newcombe Road, one of a row of working class houses in Earlsdon, Coventry. He was the eldest son of Moses and Sara Alice Whittle, Methodists who came from Lancashire. He began his education at Earlsdon Council School and according to his own estimate was "a street urchin six days of the week, and a carefully washed and dressed little boy on Sundays."

Frank showed an interest in those new-fangled flying machines at an early age – he was given a toy aeroplane, a tin Bleriot, as a Christmas present at the age of four! He saw early warplanes being manufactured at the Standard Works outside Coventry, and a big event for him as a small boy occurred when a plane made a forced landing on nearby Hearsall Common. It is said that it almost decapitated young Frank when it took off again, and his cap had to be retrieved from a gorse bush!

© Midland Air Museum

Whittle's birthplace in Earlsdon, Coventry

The family left Coventry when Frank was only nine, but he returned to Regent Street, Coventry in 1927, bringing his wife Dorothy there when they married in 1930.

LEAMINGTON

The family moved to Leamington in 1916 when his father, a skilled mechanic, used his savings and borrowed money to buy the grandly named one-man Leamington Valve and Piston Ring Company in Clinton Street. They lived at four successive houses in the town, 9 Victoria Street, 15 Church Street, 1 The Market and 18 Vincent Street.

Moses Whittle's business flourished during the War and then ran into difficulties during the subsequent recession. As a result the family had to move into poorer quality housing: in fact their last two homes are no more, those areas in Tachbrook Road and St Paul's having been redeveloped. The Whittles remained in Leamington until about 1927 after Frank had left home. They then moved to Corley Moor near the present motorway service station.

Young Frank attended Milverton Primary School in Rugby Road, and then at the age of 11 won a scholarship to Leamington College for Boys where he was a pupil from 1918 to 1923. It is said, however, that he learnt much of his engineering by studying books in Leamington Public Library in his spare time and by helping his father in his workshop.

© Warwickshire County Council

Binswood Hall Sixth Form College (Leamington College for Boys)

Well below average height, he was nicknamed 'Grub', and because of this was rather a shy boy. He was not an outstanding student; he was not keen on games; and he did not become a prefect. He is remembered as "rather a quiet reserved lad, not mixing in the kick-abouts with a ball at mid-morning and afternoon breaks." However, in those things he set his mind to he was an enthusiast. A school inspector was greatly impressed by his zeal when playing Shylock: "the zest which he displayed in sharpening his knife on his boot for his pound of flesh was terrifying to behold!" He was greatly encouraged by the science master, Major Ivor Hart, and on one occasion towards the end of his time at the school, "there was a short free period, and the boys were invited to talk to the form for ten minutes. Whittle came forward, took a piece of chalk, and held the boys fascinated for an hour. His knowledge of aircraft at that time was profound."

Even at this early age his wider view of the world is symbolised by an inscription found in one of his text books which has survived!

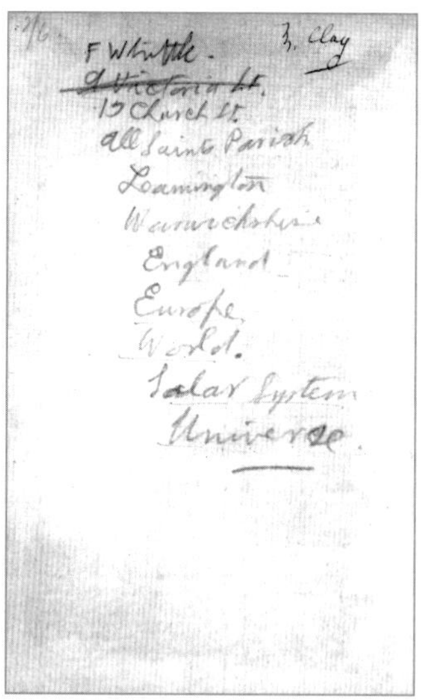

Frank Whittle's school textbook

APPRENTICESHIP AND SERVICE

Frank had always wanted to fly and was determined to join the RAF as a boy apprentice. He passed the written examination, but was turned down because he was only five feet tall. A helpful PT instructor, Sergeant Holmes, gave him a list of exercises and a diet sheet. Following these religiously, Frank added three inches to his height and three inches to his chest measurement in six months. He applied again, but was turned down on the principle of once rejected, always rejected. Here he displayed the dogged determination which was to serve him so well later on. He went through the whole procedure again as though he had never applied to enter the RAF in the first place – bureaucracy failed to notice – and he was accepted!

Full of enthusiasm 364365 Boy Whittle, F, arrived at No 4 apprenticeship wing RAF Cranwell at the tender age of sixteen to start training as a fitter. The shy lad did not exactly relish life as an apprentice. He disliked the strict discipline and coarse barrack room life, but he stuck to his studies. His main enjoyment outside training was as a member of the model aircraft society at Cranwell, in which he spent almost every spare minute available. His model making at Cranwell came to a climax when he headed a small team to build a large flying model with a 10 feet 6 inch wingspan powered by a two stroke petrol engine.

Tremendous interest was generated in the progress of the construction of this model and officers would drop in to see how things were going. Whittle, as team leader, was responsible for providing information on the project and this allowed him to reveal the depth of knowledge and wide range of skills he had acquired during his RAF training.

Whittle (right) with a Cranwell friend in the Pump Room Gardens, Leamington Spa

Whittle did so well in his three years from 1923 to 1926 at Cranwell as an apprentice, that he was one of only five transferred as a flight cadet to the RAF college there. In fact, Whittle came sixth, but number one failed his medical! A greater challenge awaited him at the college. He was one of only five working class boys among a multitude from public schools. In 1927 after thirteen and a half hours instruction, Whittle went solo in a first World War Avro 504K. A few weeks later, he was to write-off a 504 and was lucky not to be hurt in the accident. He graduated to flying the Bristol Fighter and quickly gained a reputation as something of a daredevil in low flying and aerobatics which had an irresistible appeal for Whittle.

In August 1928 Pilot Officer Whittle left his home in Coventry to report to No 111 Fighter Squadron based at Hornchurch in Essex. During his time with the Squadron he flew Armstrong Whitworth Siskins built at Coventry. He was then posted to the Central Flying School at Wittering on a three month flying instructors course. On 24th May 1930, in Coventry, while serving at No 2 Flying Training School, Digby, he married his first wife Dorothy. In June of the same year his exceptional skills as a pilot were recognised when he joined the elite to perform at the RAF Flying Pageant at Hendon.

In late 1930 he was posted to the Marine Aircraft Experimental Establishment at RAF Felixstowe as a float plane test pilot. During his time there he had many interesting experiences and one of his most exciting exploits occurred during July 1932 when he was being catapulted off HMS Ark Royal in a Fairey 111F float plane. His passenger, Flight Lieutenant Kirk, had lost his grip in the rear cockpit and bounced into the air, but he managed to grasp the fin wire and was lying on the tail plane.

Frank Whittle and his Observer during the catapulting incident on HMS Ark Royal

With difficulty Whittle brought the aeroplane in to land on the sea just missing a German liner which was crossing his path. Whittle was badly shaken but his passenger suffered no ill effects from his ordeal.

After distinguishing himself during his time as a marine test pilot Whittle was posted to RAF Henlow, in August 1932, to attend the Officer's Engineering course. On completion of his course at the end of 1933 he spent six months in charge of Aero Engine Tests at Henlow. In July 1934 he was seconded to Peterhouse College, Cambridge, where two years later – rather surprisingly because, as we shall see, he was concentrating on his work on the jet engine rather than on his academic studies – he gained First Class Honours in the Mechanical Science Tripos. A year's post-graduate studies followed, and then from 1937 to 1946 he was assigned to the Special Duty List which at last allowed him to work full time on his engine.

W2/700 Jet Aero Engine
Designed by Sir Frank Whittle and built by Power Jets Ltd., Whetstone

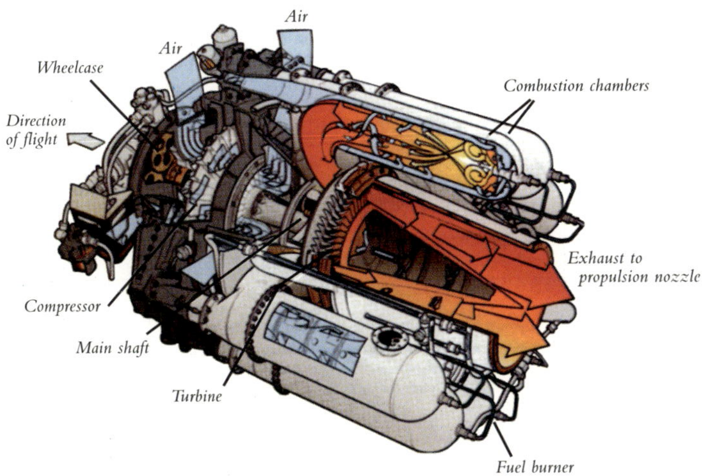

Rugby, Brownsover and the Jet Engine

However good Whittle was at aircraft acrobatics, his real interest was in aircraft propulsion. In 1928, while still at Cranwell and not yet twenty one, he had written a thesis on "Future Developments in Aircraft Design," concentrating his ideas on the engine side. He originally thought of substituting gas turbines for piston engines to drive propeller aircraft and rockets amongst others. His thinking at this time was of aircraft travelling at 500 miles per hour and at heights of 50,000 feet, but at this height a piston engine would not work, and at such speeds a propeller was hopelessly inefficient. Undaunted, he went on to consider gas turbines for jet propulsion, and it was this combination, the essential part of Whittle's engine, which would eventually power aircraft faster and higher than ever before. With this in mind, at the age of only 22, Whittle took out his first patent with the help of a friend, Pat Johnson, advocating the world's first turbo-jet. He followed this with another paper entitled "The Case for the Gas Turbine," arguing that a big increase in efficiency could be obtained with the gas turbine at great heights owing to the beneficial effects of low air temperature.

The turbine itself drives a compressor which compresses the air entering it; then the compressed air passes to a combustion chamber into which liquid fuel is injected and ignited. The gases from this combustion strike the blades of the turbine, causing it to revolve. The turbine itself works the compressor, and the gases leaving the turbine still have enough energy to provide a thrust to the rear in the form of a jey, the reaction to which propels the aircraft forward – comparable to the release of air from a blown up toy balloon.

The Air Ministry displayed no interest: according to the theories of the time Whittle's ideas were impractical. The gas turbine and compressor combination was inefficient, and the materials needed to withstand the very high temperatures and stresses required did not exist. Whittle was confident he could improve the efficiency of both the compressor and the turbine, and he was sure that the materials would evolve in the normal course of development – which they did. When in October 1930 he paid his first visit to the

British Thomson-Houston turbine factory in Rugby to discuss his turbo-jet engine project, it was to no avail. In January 1935 he allowed the patent to lapse, unable to afford the £5 renewal fee because of lack of Government support. As a result his patents were published world-wide, and appeared in the German aviation magazine "Flugsport" in the late 1930s.

Out of the blue two former RAF officers, Rolf Dudley Williams *(later Sir Rolf and MP for Exeter)* and Collingwood Tinling, offered to raise money for his research. New patents were taken out, and in March 1936 a company called Power Jets Ltd was registered with £10,000 capital. The name was chosen as being descriptive of their aims, yet unlikely to disclose them to the general public. The Air Ministry reluctantly approved, but at the same time made it clear that any work in connection with the engine was to be very much a spare-time job limited to six hours a week. It was not to conflict with Whittle's duties, namely Finals at Cambridge. Fortunately, as it turned out, his post-graduate research year and then his appointment to the Special Duty List meant that in the end he could give his full-time attention to the project for which he now proceeded to take out further patents.

Power Jets began by conducting their experiments at the British Thomson-Houston *(BTH)* factory in Rugby *(now GEC ALSTHOM)* and Whittle moved to a house called Broomfield in Bilton Road, to be near his work. This first experimental jet engine was known as the WU or Whittle Unit. It was built to Whittle's design by BTH staff on contract from Power Jets. The engine was mounted on its test truck, situated in Bay B Extension of Turbine A Building, surrounded by one inch thick steel plating as a safety precaution. A glass panel was removed from a window in the building and the jet pipe was simply pointed through it. The first test run took place on 12th April 1937.

Whittle's first experimental jet engine (WU)

© Rod Lovesey

A few seconds after Whittle started the engine, speed began to increase rapidly, the combustion chamber glowed red hot, and BTH workers, fearing an explosion, ran for cover while Whittle stayed at the controls. Fred Hudspith, a 17 year-old apprentice at the time, remembers it well. Though Whittle shut off the fuel at once, it was some time before the engine slowed down, and he later admitted to having been very frightened by the experience.

This prototype was unsuitable for powering aircraft, and Power Jets had now to develop that crude design into a reliable and much more powerful engine. To add to the technical difficulties there was a lack of Government interest and limited financial support – Whittle had to reclaim scrap metal and re-use spare parts to continue development. Air Ministry ambivalence was understandable in the circumstances. They had to concentrate on planes already in production, and with hindsight the outcome of the Battle of Britain would have been different without the Spitfires and Hurricanes then being built.

"IN ITS PRESENT STATE, AND EVEN CONSIDERING THE IMPROVEMENTS POSSIBLE WHEN ADOPTING THE HIGHER TEMPERATURES PROPOSED FOR THE IMMEDIATE FUTURE, THE GAS TURBINE ENGINE COULD HARDLY BE CONSIDERED A FEASIBLE APPLICATION TO AIRPLANES MAINLY BECAUSE OF THE DIFFICULTY IN COMPLYING WITH THE STRINGENT WEIGHT REQUIREMENTS IMPOSED BY AERONAUTICS.

"THE PRESENT INTERNAL COMBUSTION ENGINE EQUIPMENT USED IN AIRPLANES WEIGHS ABOUT 1.1 POUNDS PER HORSEPOWER, AND TO APPROACH SUCH A FIGURE WITH A GAS TURBINE SEEMS BEYOND THE REALM OF POSSIBILITY WITH EXISTING MATERIALS."

THE COMMITTEE ON GAS TURBINES
appointed by
THE NATIONAL ACADEMY OF SCIENCES
June 10, 1940

Good thing I was too stupid to know this
Frank Whittle

Whittle's comment on letter from the Committee of Gas Turbines

However, at ever speedier test runs it was becoming too dangerous to continue the experiments in an open factory, and in 1938 the testing was transferred across the County boundary to a disused BTH foundry, the Ladywood Works, at Lutterworth in Leicestershire. Local police became suspicious of Whittle's undercover activities, thinking that he might be an IRA terrorist using the premises to make bombs! As Power Jets began to recruit their own staff, they soon outgrew their small allocation of space at Lutterworth. A railway coach, on a siding nearby, had to make do as an office for the combustion engineers, and the design staff returned to Warwickshire to rent office space at Brownsover Hall, about three miles outside Rugby.

Ken Aitken's caricature of Frank Whittle (Aeroplane Monthly)

A breakthrough occurred in the summer of 1939. A previously sceptical Air Ministry official *(Dr, later Sir David Pye, the Director of Scientific Research)* was so impressed by a test run of the engine when he visited Lutterworth, that in July of that year Power Jets received a contract for the flight engine – the W1 – which Whittle was to design, and BTH were sub-contracted to manufacture. Moreover, the Air Ministry decided that the work was to go on even if war broke out. In May 1940 the Ministry authorised the manufacture of three more jet engines. This was good news *(expansion was possible)* except for the fact that the Ministry could call the tune. Power Jets were bound by the Official Secrets Act, therefore Whittle could no longer obtain money from private sources.

Whittle in conference at Brownsover Hall near Rugby in 1944

As an aeronautical engineer requiring precision, he was already experiencing difficulties with BTH staff who thought in terms of massive weight: as he put it, "It was a bit like expecting the makers of Big Ben to make a good job of a ladies' wrist watch." Now the Ministry wanted the Rover Company involved in his project as well *(Rolls Royce later took over from Rover)*. If BTH had no previous experience of aero-engines Rover had no previous experience of turbo-type machinery whatsoever. Whittle was required to hand over information to both companies without any safeguards. As he himself wrote in his autobiography "Jet," "To the other two firms, the turbo-jet was only a minor part of their total activities, whereas it was Power Jets' sole raison d'être. We depended entirely on it, and since we were wholly financed by the Ministry at this stage, our survival as a team hung on a very delicate thread. The Power Jets' team was now a very real thing, and I believe that it was only its high quality and its continuing record of achievement that saved it from extinction at an early stage."

THE JET PLANE

The Ministry had given the contract to build the prototype jet plane to the Gloster Aircraft Company back in July 1939. In April 1941 their chief test pilot Gerry Sayer put the single-engined Gloster/Whittle E28/39 *(powered by the experimental W1X engine)* through its taxiing trials at Hucclecote, near Gloucester, actually achieving three hops of 200-300 yards in the process. Whittle also taxied the E28/39. The aircraft was then moved to RAF Cranwell for its maiden flight. On 15th May 1941, at 7.35pm watched by Frank Whittle and the aircraft's designer George Carter, Sayer taxied the aircraft to the end of the long Cranwell runway and with the canopy open he took off for the very first time. Powered by the purpose-designed W1 flight engine, the aircraft flew for some 17 minutes before making a perfect landing back at Cranwell. An aeroplane had flown without a propeller! *(The E28 and W1 engine are now in the Science Museum, London and the W1X engine in the Smithsonian Museum, Washington, but one of the later W2/700 engines is on display locally at the Midland Air Museum at Baginton.)*

© Barry James

W2/700 start up to celebrate 50th Anniversary of Cranfield University in June 1996

The first flight passed off without any official recognition and the Air Ministry could not even be persuaded to send an official photographic unit to record this significant event! The only record of the first flight was made by a hand held film camera and one or two still photographs taken at the end of the flight showing Whittle congratulating Sayer. A few days later Air Ministry big-wigs came to see it, and then later trials were conducted over Warwickshire's Edgehill where King and Parliament had fought three centuries before. When Churchill was later shown a demonstration flight he was duly impressed by the aircraft's performance and the accompanying Spitfires just could not keep up with the jet plane!

E28/39 Whittle Jet over Edgehill, Warwickshire. June 1942
Painting by Ken Aitken

In the interests of the war effort the secret was shared with the United States. In the autumn of 1941 a dismantled jet engine was flown over the Atlantic in the bomb bay of a Liberator. This Anglo-American sharing of secrets was carried out before America's entry into the war in December 1941. The General Electric Company of America got to work on the design and impressed Whittle with their speed and enthusiasm when he flew over to advise in the summer of 1942. The American's first jet plane, the Aerocomet, flew within a year, less than eighteen months after the British plane. They were really keen, and Whittle was left wishing he had received such co-operation in England a few years earlier! The development of aero gas turbines had been entirely due to Whittle's foresight and determination, and America was virtually given a free passport into this new and exciting form of propulsion.

Due to the engine problems and unnecessary political factors mentioned later, the first Gloster Meteor jet fighter was not delivered to the RAF until May 1944. The twin engined Meteors were initially used to shoot down V1 flying-bombs, which were terrorising London and the South Coast of England. In the closing stages of the war Meteors of 616 Squadron were sent to Belgium to seek out German jet fighters, but in the event no encounters took place.

© Midland Air Museum

Early prototype Meteor surrounded by pilot and ground crew

Whittle did not fly a jet plane himself until October 1945. He was banned from doing so because his expertise was regarded as too valuable to risk. He then flew from Bruntingthorpe in Leicestershire in a Meteor fitted with engines manufactured by Power Jets, and he was proud to be the only person apart from the Wright brothers to fly an aircraft with a power plant he had designed himself.

Production of the Meteor ceased in 1955 after nearly four thousand had been built, including over one thousand constructed by Armstrong Whitworth in Whittle country at Baginton.

When peace came Britain pioneered the development of the world's first jet airliner, the De Havilland Comet powered by four De Havilland Ghost engines, but due to technical problems with the aircraft, the initiative in aircraft technology, to Whittle's sorrow, soon passed to the United States with Boeing taking the lead in long range jet travel, although Britain retained a leading role in jet engine development.

THE RISE AND FALL OF POWER JETS

With the demands of the Ministry of Aircraft Production, Power Jets had continued to expand. Outgrowing its Lutterworth site, the works had moved again in 1942 yet farther from Warwickshire to Whetstone, near Leicester, which may have been the first purpose built factory in the world to build jet engines. The staff continued to rise to well over a thousand – a far cry from the days when Whittle and the one other employee shared the typing! In January 1944 the whole jet achievement was announced to the world. Whittle thought it premature, as the Germans then became aware of Britain's developments, but it had a morale building propaganda value and Group Captain Whittle became a household name overnight.

Power Jets Factory at Whetstone 1943

It was by no means all sweetness and light. Whittle was never to be given complete control of his brain-child. The Air Ministry had decided that Power Jets was not to manufacture the final product, but merely to research experimental engines. The actual mass production of the W2B engines for the Meteor had been given to Rover. Whittle had intended that Rover should be the sub-contractor, but unknown to Whittle the firm went to the Air Ministry and in effect, having acquired all his secrets, became his competitor. Moreover, while Rover were allowed to make minor alterations where necessary to assist with production, they proceeded – erroneously – to carry out major changes in design. This led to a situation in which the two parties involved, Rover and Power Jets, no longer had a working relationship and this delayed production of the engine. During this period a chain of events had been set in motion which would eventually lead to Rover handing over their jet engine work to Rolls Royce and towards the end of 1942 the final agreement was sealed over a pub meal with Ernest Hives, Stanley Hooker of Rolls Royce and Spencer Wilkes of Rover at the Swan and Royal Hotel in Clitheroe. This weakened Power Jets position still further. EW *(later Lord)* Hives of Rolls-Royce, whom Whittle described as "an honest rogue who told you he was going to do the dirty beforehand," declared, "We're the centre of the job, and nothing you can do will stop us." To add insult to injury, in April 1944 Power Jets, but no other gas-turbine firm, was nationalised. The other firms were left to their own devices. Whittle's vision of a completely nationalised gas-turbine industry with Power Jets at the top of the pyramid evaporated.

A major project being carried out by Power Jets during this period was work on the engine for the Miles M52 Supersonic aircraft which was designed to travel at speeds of 1,000 mph. When first conceived in 1944, the aircraft was ahead of its time and would have put Britain in the forefront of supersonic flight. The engine to power this aircraft would have been Whittle's latest design, the W2/700, plus a Turbo-Fan *(Frank Whittle's 1936 Patent)* fitted to the rear with after burning/reheat. The engine was completed and ran in 1946 at Whetstone, but the aircraft and engine were cancelled and it was left to the Americans to break the sound barrier with the Bell X1 aircraft.

© Midland Air Museum

Miles M52 W2/700 engine on test, Whetstone July 1945, Whittle in RAF uniform

Invention was one thing, but all this protracted negotiation with 'big brother' firms and unpredictable government departments took its toll on Whittle's health and he had to have several spells off work in hospital or convalescing. Finally, a disappointed man, he resigned in January 1946 from the revamped Power Jets. Whittle was only interested in research as a necessary adjunct to development, and not as an end in itself to which the firm was now limited. Indeed, he would have resigned earlier but had stayed put because he did not want to be accused of breaking up the government company. The jet age proceeded without its creator.

Due to ill-health Whittle retired from the RAF in April 1948, with the rank of Air Commodore, after 25 years service. The following month he received an ex gratia award of £100,000 free of tax on the recommendation of the Royal Commission on Awards to Inventors *(some of which he characteristically passed on to his colleagues).* The month after that he was made a Knight Commander of the Order of the British Empire in the Birthday Honours List.

The German Rivals

It is true that there was no need to resort to jet air combat in the Second World War, but Britain would have been in dire need of Whittle's invention if the war had lasted a year or two longer. Little was known about the German jet programme. The German Hans Von Ohain fired a jet engine a few months after Whittle: the experimental Heinkel HE 178 jet flew before the Whittle E 28/39: and the Messerschmitt ME 262 was on active service in the closing stages of the war. Fortunately for the Allies, Hitler had originally decreed that the ME 262 should be used as a fighter bomber and not as a fighter which greatly impaired its operational use. Whittle's philosophy was slow but sure and accurate; German researchers and designers, out of desperation with the war being lost, were out for quick rather than accurate results. Once in the air the ME 262s could be effective because of their speed and only the lack of enough skilled pilots and fuel stopped them doing greater damage to the allied bomber formations which were roaming over Germany. However, the allied fighter pilots had perfected the art of catching the German jet fighters as they were taking off and landing at their bases during which time they were vulnerable to attack. Their reliability was poor and one ME 262 unit lost 23 pilots in accidents in the space of three months.

Retirement

Although Whittle was disillusioned by the treatment he had received over the years from the authorities, retirement from the RAF did not mean a life of inactivity. His energies were transferred from military to civil aviation, from wartime engineering to peaceful applications of the science. He immediately became a Technical Adviser to the British Overseas Airways Corporation, one of the forerunners of British Airways, and helped to plan their Comet Jetliner operations. Later in the 1960s he was Technical Adviser to Bristol Siddeley Engines, developing the radical Whittle Turbodrill for drilling through the earth's crust.

Sir Frank became a jetsetter himself on busy lecture tours. In 1976 he emigrated to the United States where he had married his second wife Hazel, a former nurse and air stewardess. He became Navair Research Professor at the US Naval Academy in Annapolis, and pursued a busy schedule of consulting and lecturing from his home in Columbia, Maryland.

It was a source of great pride to him that his son Ian became a senior jet captain with Cathay Pacific Airways.

Plentiful recognition in the second half of his life helped Sir Frank to forget the lack of it during the first half when he was struggling to interest the powers that be in his ideas. He always denied any bitterness and acknowledged instead his immense debt to his beloved Royal Air Force and Great Britain.

Sir Frank Whittle died at his Maryland home on 8th August 1996 at the age of 89, losing a long battle against cancer. A memorial service in Westminster Abbey was held in his honour the following November.

© Barry James

Ian Whittle and a Power Jet W2/700 engine at Farnborough Air Show in September 1996

Honours

When the extent of Whittle's invention had become known, honours were showered upon him. In 1944 he was made a Commander of the Order of the British Empire; two years later he became a commander of the US Legion of Merit: in 1947 he was made a Companion of the Order of the Bath and as already mentioned, in June 1948 he was knighted as a KBE. Very belatedly, in 1986, he was invested by the Queen with the Order of Merit, the highest award in the gift of the Sovereign which confers no title and is limited to 24 of the most distinguished people in the country.

He received honorary doctorates from eleven universities and numerous fellowships and medals from learned societies. These included the Fellowship of the Royal Society and the Honorary Fellowship and Gold Medal of the Royal Aeronautical Society. He also received many overseas honours and awards, especially from the USA. These included the Guggenheim Medal, the Benjamin Franklin Medal and the Goddard Medal, and he shared the Charles Draper Award with Von Ohain.

It is also pleasing to know that he was honoured in his native Warwickshire. One of the doctorates was from the University of Warwick.

The Whittle Inheritance

In October 1997 the Sound Barrier and World Land Speed record were broken by a British designed and built vehicle, Thrust SSC almost fifty years to the day since the Bell XI Aircraft broke the sound barrier for the first time. This vehicle was powered by two Rolls Royce Spey aircraft engines, and supported by many Coventry and Warwickshire companies. The driver was RAF pilot Flight Lieutenant Andy Green who was born in Atherstone, Warwickshire. This great British achievement would not have been possible without Whittle's invention of the jet engine.

Memories of Whittle

There is a road called Whittle Croft in outer Birmingham a little to the north of Junction 5 on the M6. Coventry conferred an Award of Merit and named a primary school in Woodway Lane and a street, Whittle Close in Binley, after him. The Midland Air Museum at Baginton was responsible in June 1982 for placing a plaque on the house in Earlsdon where he was born and for opening the Sir Frank Whittle Jet Heritage Centre at the Museum itself in 1987. The Sir Frank Whittle Business Centre in Rugby is named after him, and there is a Whittle Close in the town. In Leamington the "Jet and Whittle" public house in Brunswick Street bears his name. There is another "Jet and Whittle" in Gloucester, the home of the aircraft powered by the Whittle engine. There is also a Whittle Court in Leamington, a residence for the elderly.

In his halcyon days Sir Frank paid three official return visits to Leamington: in October 1944 to receive the Freedom of the Borough; in May 1945 to distribute the prizes on Speech Day as the most distinguished Old Boy of Leamington College; and in July 1952 to be present when a plaque to his memory was unveiled in the school hall. He also served as President of the Old Leamingtonians' Association. A Sir Frank Whittle Craftsman Prize was awarded annually. One gentlemen who gained it in 1950 still makes use of his furniture manual today.

Just across the County boundary in Lutterworth a road, a pub, and a block of flats for senior citizens bear his name and a bronze bust of Whittle was erected in the town gardens. British Airways named a Boeing 777 in his honour. In 1991 the GPO commemorated the 50th anniversary of the first flight of Sir Frank's jet engine when it issued a set of stamps dedicated to pioneers of science: one of the four showed the Gloster/Whittle E28/39 flying over eastern England. Also a current series of stamps illustrating aircraft includes the Meteor. Finally, one of the main halls in the Queen Elizabeth II Conference Centre in London is named after him.

GEC ALSTHOM

The association between Sir Frank Whittle and GEC ALSTHOM, through its predecessor companies, began in 1936 when Power Jets Ltd, the company formed by Whittle and colleagues to develop the first jet engine, was set up on the GEC ALSTHOM site in Rugby.

GEC ALSTHOM is a world leader in the design, manufacture and commissioning of equipment and systems for the power generation, power transmission and distribution and rail transportation industries.

GEC ALSTHOM's Engineering Systems company and its Mechanical Engineering Centre are located at Whetstone, near Leicester, on the site where the Power Jets' factory was built to test and produce the first jet engine. The Whetstone site has continued its association with the aircraft industry through the provision of automated passenger checking systems; baggage and cargo handling equipment; aircraft docking guidance systems; and aircraft engine development, test and maintenance facilities. Whetstone is also the location for the Whittle Test Centre, a new facility dedicated to the development and testing of power generation technologies.

Another GEC ALSTHOM company in the UK, European Gas Turbines in Lincoln, is also linked with Sir Frank Whittle. In 1946, engineers from Power Jets joined the Company to begin work on the first industrial gas turbine. Now, EGT is one of the world's leading industrial and aircraft gas turbine manufacturers.

GEC ALSTHOM is proud of its association with Sir Frank Whittle, and through its current businesses and technologies, the legacy of a great man continues to make its mark throughout the world.

GEC ALSTHOM

BUSINESS CENTRE

A few hundred yards from the spot where Whittle conducted much of his pioneering work in the BTH works *(now GEC ALSTHOM),* in April 1937, is the Sir Frank Whittle Business Centre opened in 1994 by Lord Prior on the Great Central Industrial Estate. Owned and managed by Warwickshire County Council, the Centre provides purpose built units to enable businesses to develop their potential in a prestigious, inexpensive, professional environment. The project is one of the initiatives of the County Council which encourages the development of new businesses in Warwickshire.

The Business Centre is two miles from Junction 1 of the M6 motorway. Rugby railway station, which has a mainline InterCity service to London, Euston, *(55 minutes travel time)*, is within a few minutes walk. It can be accessed by tenants twenty four hours a day, and provides all the support facilities which a modern business requires. The letting policy enables businesses to leave at one month's notice so that occupants do not have to commit to a burdensome lease agreement.

A new Business Resource Centre is planned which will be available to unit holders as well as local businesses. With the support of partners it is envisaged that Sir Frank Whittle Business Centre will become established as the Centre for business support in Rugby.

For further information telephone: 01788 551500.

ACKNOWLEDGEMENTS

The author acknowledges with thanks all who have helped him in any way, especially Roy Fowkes who made helpful suggestions on reading the original draft; Frederick Hudspith, formerly of British Thomson-Houston; and Ken Hathway, Works Manager of GEC ALSTHOM. He has also consulted the Whittle Papers in the Archives Centre at Churchill College, Cambridge, and other material provided by the Warwickshire County Record Office and the Modern Records Centre at the University of Warwick.

Edited by Merle Bayliss with special thanks to Barry James, Chairman of the Board of Trustees of the Midland Air Museum, for devoting so much time to this publication. He has added a new dimension to the biography and has provided a unique source of additional information, illustrations and photographs from the archives of the Museum.

This publication is part of the joint work of Warwickshire County & Rugby Borough Councils commemorating Whittle's association with his home county.

THE MIDLAND AIR MUSEUM

The Museum houses a unique collection of aircraft, engines and supporting exhibits in the Sir Frank Whittle Jet Heritage Centre illustrating the fascinating story of Sir Frank Whittle and the jet age.

The Museum is ideally suited to educational visits by school parties or other organised groups. Further information can be obtained on telephone: 01203 301033.

© Barry James

Power Jets W2/700 engine on display in the Sir Frank Whittle Jet Heritage Centre at the Midland Air Museum

Cover illustration: Young Whittle's experience on Hearsall Common,
original sketch by Ken Aitken for this publication
Cover photographs: © Midland Air Museum
Other photographs and illustrations: © as indicated

Design and layout by Steven Lippert, County Graphics